THE INTELLIGENT DESIGN
COLORING BOOK

Soft Skull Press
an imprint of

COUNTERPOINT | BERKELEY

Cover text design by Sharon McGill
Printed in the United States of America
ISBN 978-1-59376-409-8

Intelligent Design Books
A division of Mega-Pheasant Heights Graphics
www.intelligentdesigncoloringbook.com

In conjunction with

Soft Skull Press
An Imprint of Counterpoint LLC
1919 Fifth Street
Berkeley, CA 94710

www.softskull.com
www.counterpointpress.com

Distributed by Publishers Group West

10 9 8 7 6 5 4 3

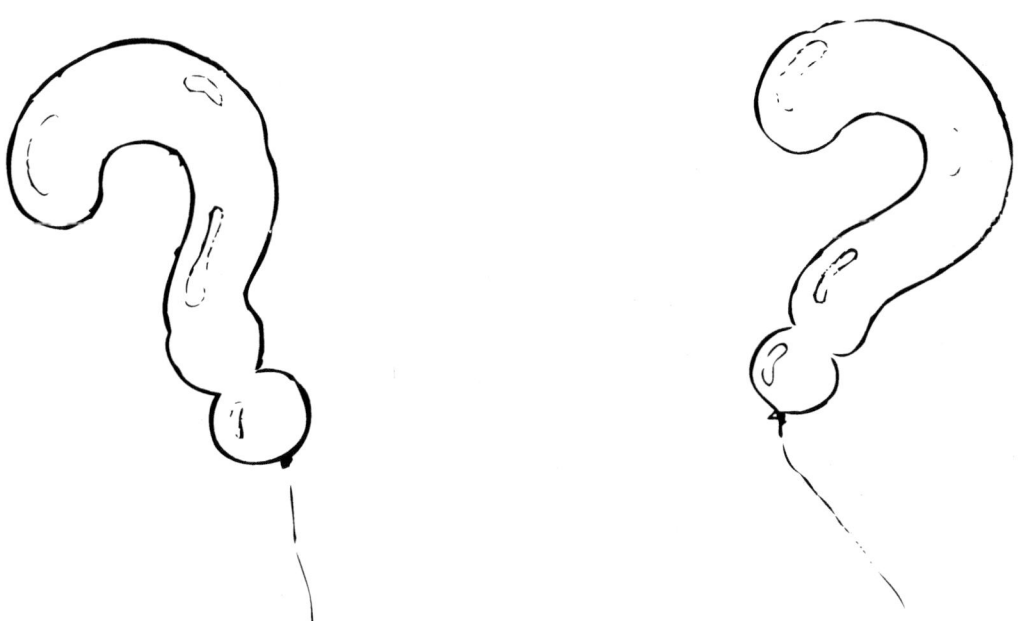

This coloring book is dedicated to Dr. James Dobson who inspired the deep, spiritual thought and royalty structure that made it possible.

✦ SUNDAY SCHOOL ✦
CAN BE FUN

To celebrate my tenth anniversary of teaching Sunday school at the Mega-Pheasant Heights Assembly Church, I've put together the *Intelligent Design Coloring Book* to help you learn about the concept of the Intelligent Designer. Stacey Schlemmer (the cookie lady from the Lake Seneca retreat) did the drawings, and I wrote the words. Thanks for all your hard work, Stacey!

The relationship between God, the Holy Spirit and the Intelligent Designer is a mysterious one which cannot be fully explained in logical terms. That's what mysterious means.

Though we discourage you from questioning our beliefs, you have a way of not following directions. So, to address some common misunderstandings and to tackle some of your questions, we put together a coloring book that makes you think! But not too much. Sometimes difficult questions have very simple answers.

We included activities, coloring pages, drawings, cut-and-pastes, and brain ticklers because learning about our wondrous universe can be just as entertaining as it is educational.

Because of the confirmation incident with Scooter Norquist, we no longer allow questioning of scripture out loud. But we do encourage you to submit your written questions to our Inquisition Box. We've published some of the more important ones in these pages.

Just the other day, Ashley Staveredes (13) asked me how there could be so many different religions. "How can they all be right?" It was an excellent question.

Let's turn the page to find the answer.

✦ SO MANY FAITHS ✦

Though there are so many religions, there's only one right one. And it's ours. That doesn't mean that we don't have to respect other people's religions. It just means they're wrong and we need to teach them the truth. We must always remember to do this with humility. When the Intelligent Designer told everyone else how to live and said the only way to Truth was through Him, he was humble about it.

We hope this activity book will help increase your knowledge of our fascinating universe and reduce its complexity into simple, easy-to-understand answers that even a child with no education can appreciate.

Faith is available to everyone. Education isn't.

Amen!

Pastor Brett

✦ THE RIGHT FAITH ✦

The people on the ground have faith in the Intelligent Designer and pray to him but unfortunately they do not have the right faith. The pilot has the right faith.

The difference between believing in the right faith and the wrong faith can be significant.

Turn the page to find out.

✦ THE WRONG FAITH ✦

While you're coloring in these pieces, take a moment to pray for these people who didn't get a chance to know how truly comforting the one true Intelligent Designer's grace and boundless love can be.

✦ TOLERANCE AND ✦ UNDERSTANDING

The Intelligent Designer wants us to be tolerant and sensitive to people who are different from us. Before you share the Truth with someone about the only one true Intelligent Designer, it is important to be respectful of that person's beliefs.

1) Connect the dots on the opposite page to see the Intelligent Designer of Islam.

2) Go on the internet and find a pen-pal in the Middle East.

3) Ask your new pen pal to draw a picture of your Intelligent Designer.

4) Exchange your drawings.

✦ FAITH AND SCIENCE ✦

Some people are not blessed by the grace of the Intelligent Designer because they don't have faith. It's sad. Just imagine what it would be like to see the world through their science eyes. Cut out these science glasses, tie a string around them, and put them on.

Now imagine a world without faith. Where people don't have any houses of worship. They don't have Bibles or Korans or Sunday school. They just walk around having fun, drinking, dancing, eating, watching TV and reading whatever interests them, rather than the Bible. It's very sad. It's okay to cry for them.

Now take off the glasses and open your eyes. Do you see the light? Can you feel the Intelligent Designer's grace washing over your soul like fabric softener relaxing a stiff pair of underpants in the laundry?

The grace of the Intelligent Designer, that relaxed fit of your soul, is only available to people who have faith in Him more than in science or their own thoughts or interests.

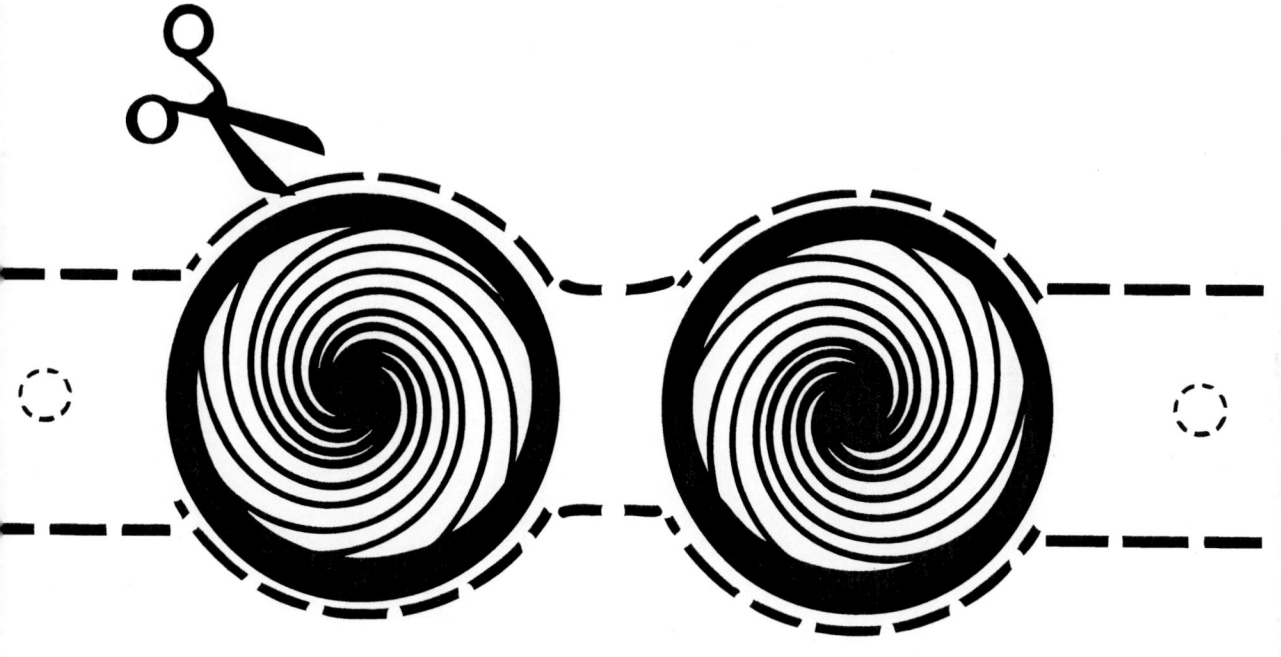

15

✦ INTELLIGENT DESIGN ✦
v.
EVOLUTION

Look at the opposite page.

Paul and Lisa both have baskets. Paul has the [basket: EVOLUTION] and Lisa has the [basket: INTELLIGENT DESIGN]

Cut out the eggs and paste them in Lisa's basket if they support <u>intelligent design</u> or Paul's basket if they support <u>evolution</u>.

(turn the page for the solution)

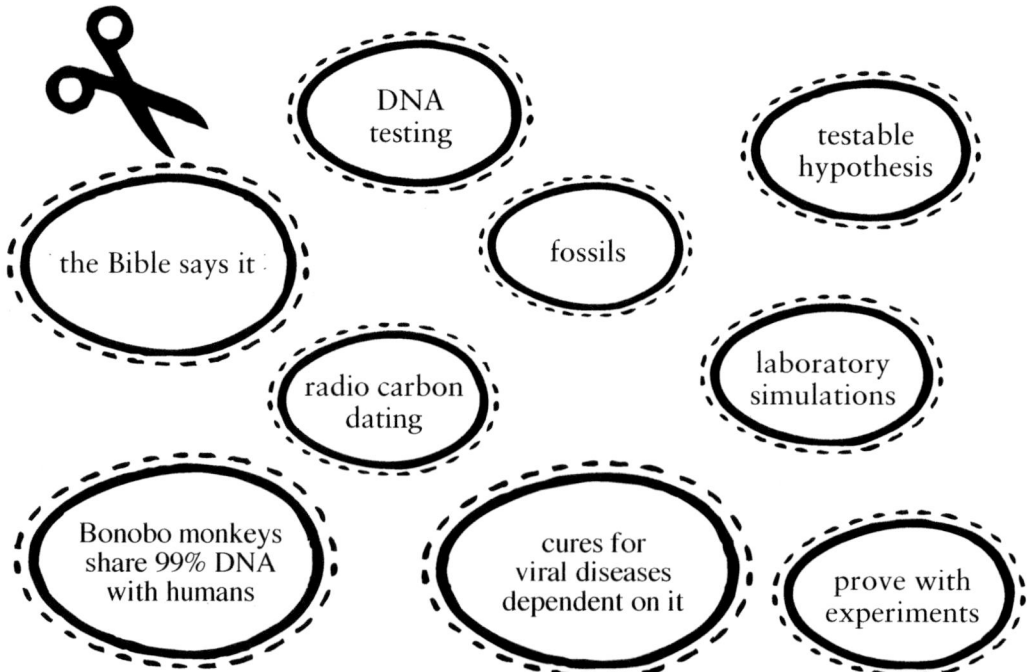

DNA testing

testable hypothesis

the Bible says it

fossils

radio carbon dating

laboratory simulations

Bonobo monkeys share 99% DNA with humans

cures for viral diseases dependent on it

prove with experiments

Look, Paul's basket is so full, he can't even pick it up or he'll break his eggs. But Lisa's basket is so light she can skip with it.

That's faith.

It makes our soul so light it's like skipping through life with an almost empty basket.

✦ HE SEES EVERYTHING ✦

Oh no! Look what the Intelligent Designer has caught in his telescope.

The Intelligent Designer is very interested in homosexual activity. Wars, torture, floods, starvation, flat tires, smoking—none of these are as important to him. Any time homosexuals engage in homosexual behavior, he's watching. Very closely. It really bothers him. It's probably exhausting for him because he has to watch it ALL the time. Especially in New York. He can't afford to take his eyes off it.

It's wrong to engage in homosexual activity because it distracts the Intelligent Designer from more important problems.

That's why many bad things that happen in the world are homosexuals' fault.

✦ HE THOUGHT OF ✦ EVERYTHING

On this page you get to pretend to be the Intelligent Designer and design the world the way you want it.

Before you do your drawing, think about how you would design it.

Hmmmm.

Keep thinking.

It's impossible, isn't it? How could you do a better job than the Intelligent Designer?

He's thought of everything. Think about all the weapons he has given us to help fight our violent enemies.

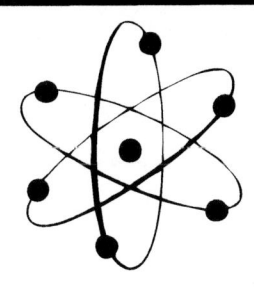

✦ MEET MONSIEUR ✦ FONTENOT™

Monsieur Fontenot™ is everyone's favorite rodent. He helps us learn how to make good decisions.

He really wants that cheese. How's he going to succeed?

Sometimes, when something seems so hard, we turn to prayer to help us surmount difficult obstacles.

Color the cheese YELLOW, his jacket and shoes RED, his pants and hat BLACK, and his fur GREY. While you're coloring, take the time to pray with him.

When you're finished, turn the page for a surprise.

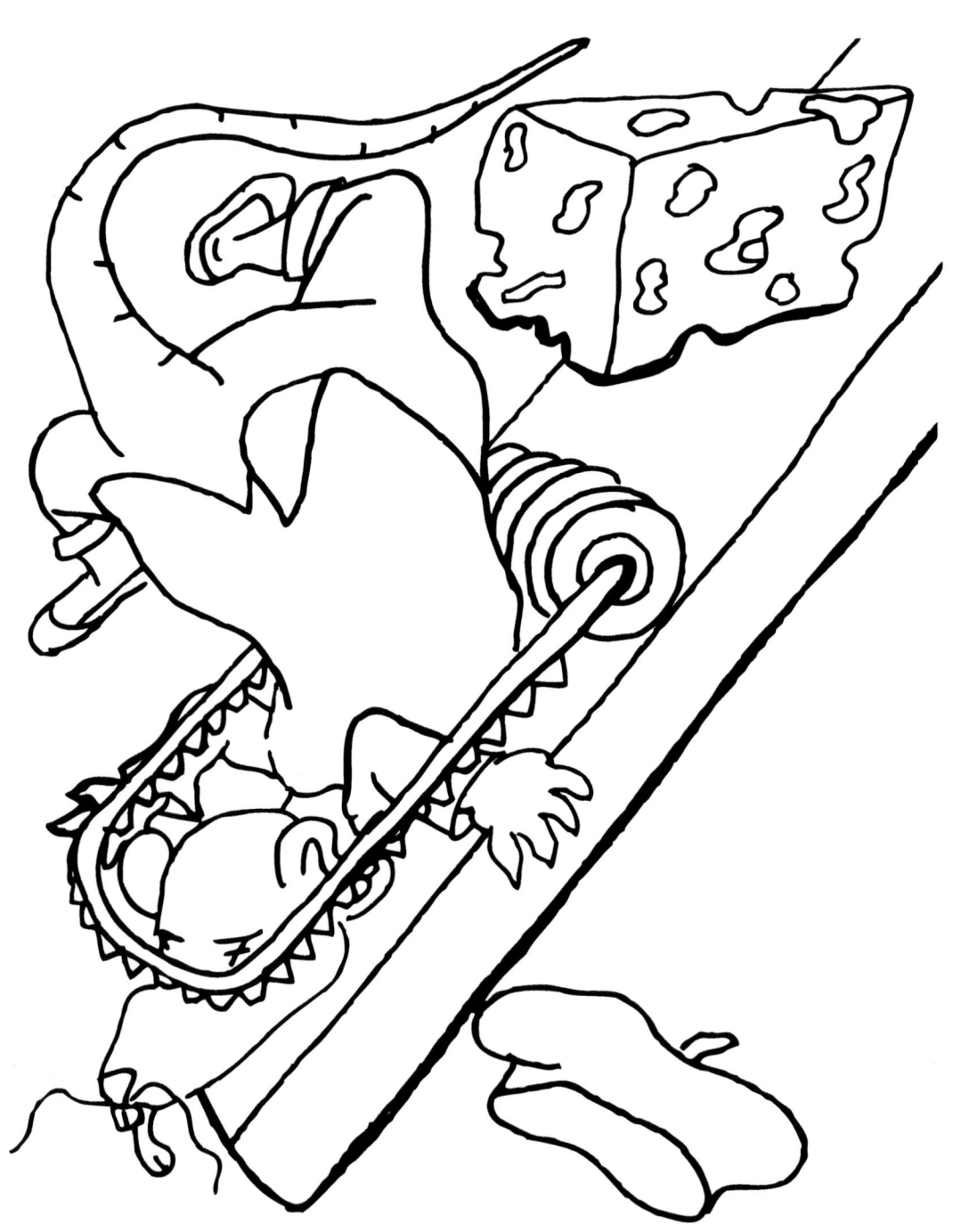

An important lesson.

✦ THE POWER OF FAITH ✦

Our prayers are not always answered. In fact, not very often. Almost never, really. But that doesn't mean He doesn't care or He isn't listening.

But you know what? We don't need to be sad for Monsieur Fontenot™ because if he believed in the Intelligent Designer, he went to Heaven to be with Him for eternity. And that's plenty of time to eat all the cheese he wants.

If you have faith you can never, ever be proven wrong. And do you know what's better than always being right?

NOTHING!

✦ MUTUALLY EXCLUSIVE ✦ PRAYERS

What if two people pray for opposite things? How can both their prayers come true?

Aaron Richards (12)
West Nyack, New York

Wow. That's a very smart question, Aaron. Are you sure you're not Jewish? LOL. Study the opposite page.

Sometimes prayers are *mutually exclusive*. This is a fancy way of saying that it's impossible for both fish to have their prayers answered at the same time.

Why?

It's because of the *mysterious* nature of *spirituality*. Rather than think about this and get frustrated (that's called philosophy), let's use the bright colors the Intelligent Designer designed for us and color in the fish.

Color them RED, WHITE, and BLUE. Like our flag.

✤ EVERYONE PRAYS ✤

When Muslims pray, they say "Allah Akbar," which means "God is Great."

When we pray, we say "praise be to God," which means "praise be to God."

That proves the Intelligent Designer is everywhere! For some reason, on this day, he answered the prayers of the people flying the planes.

Maybe it was because of something bad you did. While you're coloring in the opposite page, think about what you might have done to make Him so angry.

The Intelligent Designer is everywhere.

✦ TELEVISION ✦

Q: If the Intelligent Designer wants to tell us what to do so badly, why doesn't he get his own TV show?

Jeremy McCracken (9)
Baton Rouge, Louisiana

A: That's an excellent question, Jeremy. It's because the Jews, the gays, and the liberals control the television and they won't let him have one.

Though the Intelligent Designer it powerful, he's no match for the Jews, the gays, and the liberals when they team up.

What would the Intelligent Designer's show look like? Draw it on the empty screen.

✦ SYMBOLS ✦

A *symbol* is a material object used to represent something invisible.

Identify and circle the religious *symbols* on the next page.

Did you know?

Killing is always wrong. But sometimes it's not. Like when a President tells you to do it. That's called a war. And then it's okay.

Amen!

(solution)

✦ IT'S IMPOSSIBLE ✦

Some activist scientists want us to believe that all life evolved from a common ancestor.

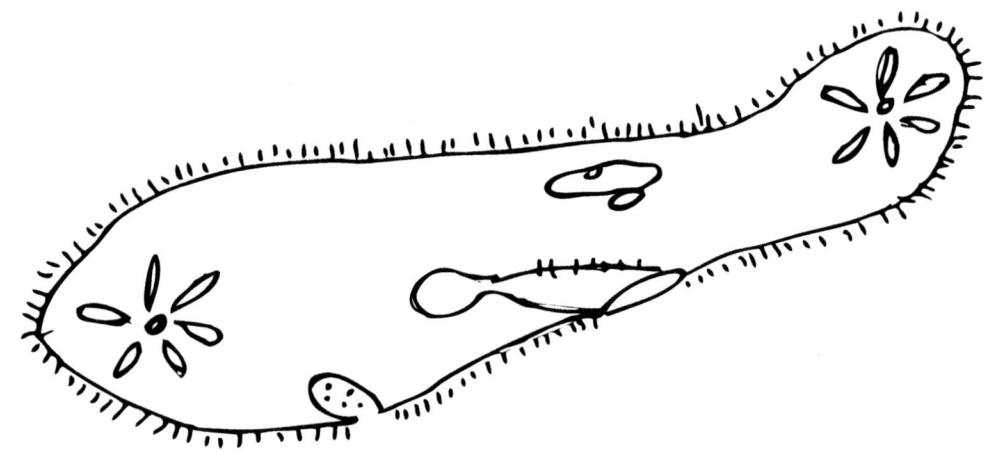

But how is this possible?

The *slug* and the *aardvark* couldn't possibly be related.

See how different they look?

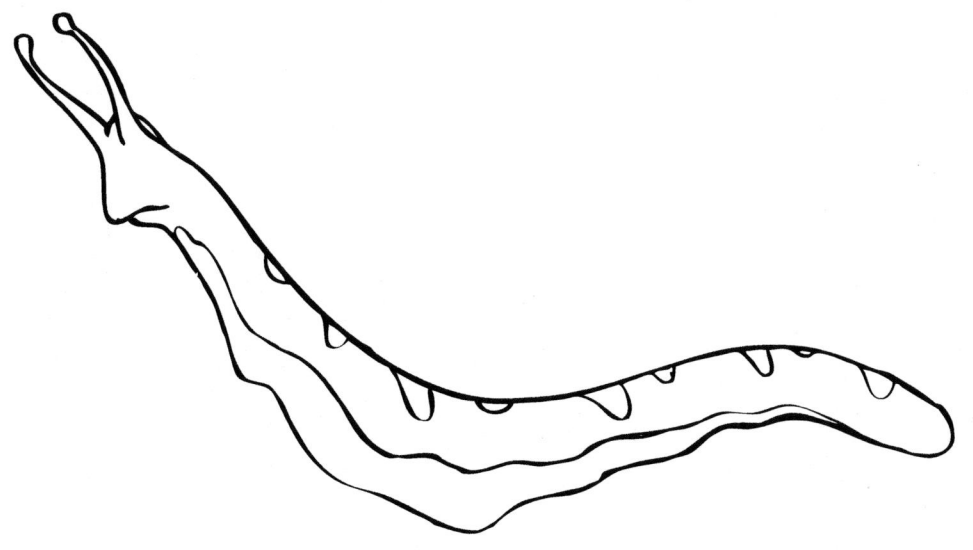

✦ LET'S NOT BE WEIRD ✦

Look at the opposite page. These parts of our face are not in the order the Intelligent Designer designed for us. They look weird, don't they?

Cut them out and arrange them intelligently so they don't look weird.

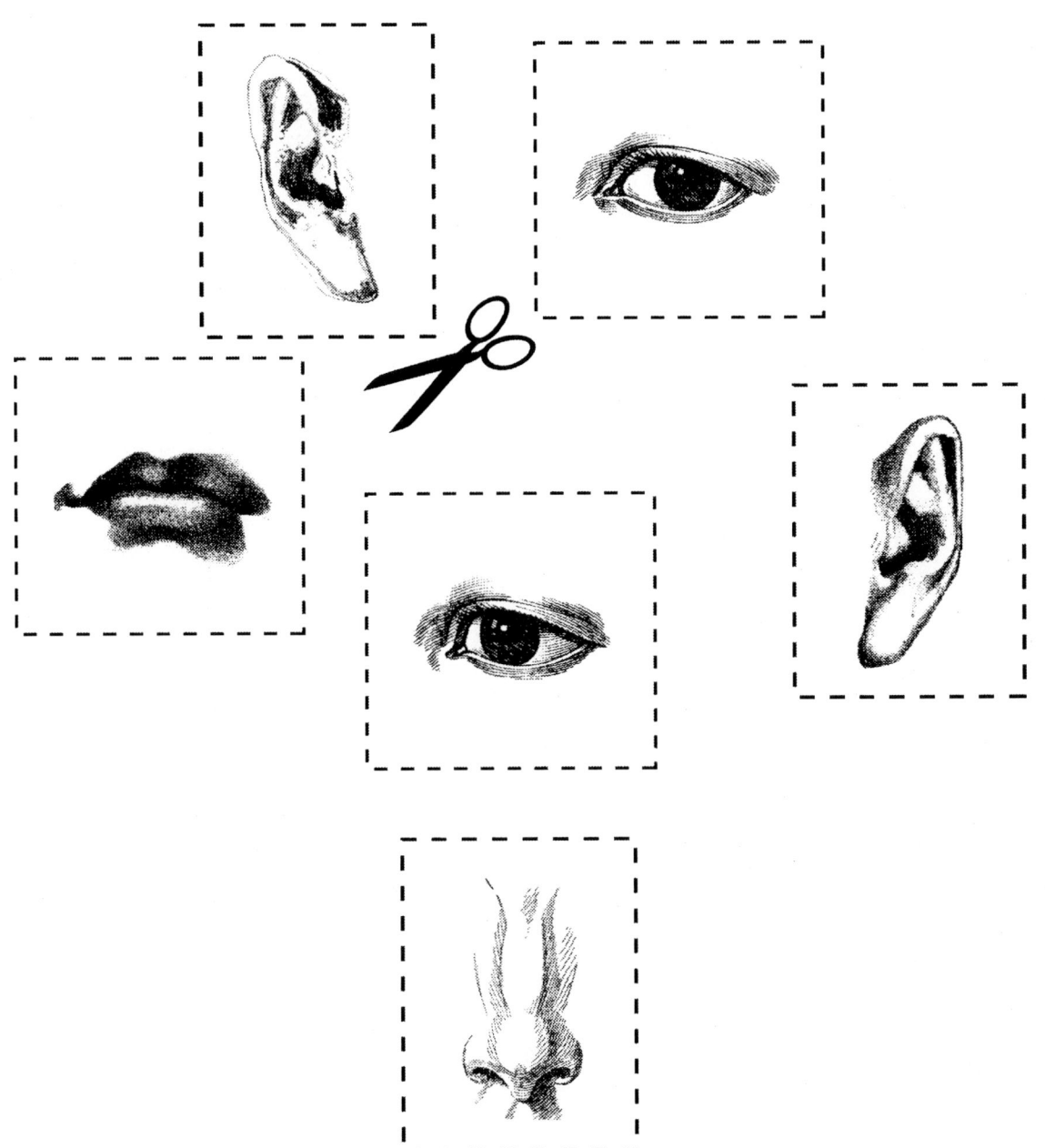

✦ PEOPLE AND MONKEYS ✦
ARE DIFFERENT

Scientists and reality-based thinkers would like us to believe that people evolved from monkeys.

But people and monkeys are very different.

Compare these two pages.

Circle all the ways people
and monkeys are different.

✦ THE INTELLIGENT ✦ DESIGNER'S WORK

Carrie is doing the Intelligent Designer's work. Using her breasts, she attempts to distract Matt from looking at Michael.

Breasts can be used for good or evil. When they're used to foil homosexual activity, it pleases the Intelligent Designer.

To celebrate her success, color her bathing suit PINK because she's a girl and Matt and Michael's bathing suits BLUE because they're boys.

✦ FREE WILL ✦

Mr. Burwick explains free will to Mr. King.

The Intelligent Designer gave us *free will*, which is a beautiful thing except when you don't follow His rules. So even though you have free will, you have to make choices that please Him. Which means you don't have free will.

Also, he has a *plan* for us, which means you don't have free will because no matter what you do, you're just fulfilling his plan.

But you have free will.

Use a white crayon to color in Mr. Burwick and Mr. King.

✦ COINCIDENCE? ✦

MUSLIMS believe that Allah ordered the angels to go to earth and bring back seven handfuls of soil, all of different colors, from which he could create human beings.

ANCIENT GREEKS believed that the god Prometheus molded human beings from clay.

THE MIK'MAQ INDIANS of Nova Scotia believed the god Gisoolg caused a bolt of lightening to form the image of a human being from sand.

THE COMMANCHE INDIANS believed that the Great Spirit collected swirls of dust to create their people.

JEWS AND CHRISTIANS believe Yahweh formed man from the dust of the ground and breathed life into his nostrils.

✦ PROOF! ✦

All over the world, great peoples believe the same thing. The Intelligent Designer made humans out of dirt and magically brought them to life.

Coincidence?

Of course not!

This is proof of just how intelligent He truly is. He can make human beings out of mud.

You can't do that, can you?

✦ LOVE AND SCIENCE ✦

Though scientists have tried many times, they have not been able to create love in a laboratory.

WARNING:

IF YOU ARE NOT OLD ENOUGH TO BE IN MRS. BIGELOW'S CONFIRMATION CLASS, YOU MUST TURN TO THE LAST PAGE.

✦ RELATIONS ✦

Even though the Intelligent Designer designed us to want to have relations with lots of different people, he gets really sad when you have relations with lots of different people. We don't know why this is. It seems more intelligent to design us to only have relations with the person who we marry but who are we to try and understand His intelligence?

If you never find someone to marry, you shouldn't have relations. Even if this makes you unhappy. He doesn't care about what makes you happy. He cares about you following his rules. That makes Him happy. And isn't that what it's all about. Making Him happy?

It's so disrespectful to question His commands or His decisions. Who do you think you are?

Anyway, do you know the names of the people on the next page? It's _ _ _ _ and _ _ _ .

Because they didn't listen to the Intelligent Designer, we all have to suffer. While you color in the page, think about suffering. And relations.

✤ WHY RELATIONS? ✤

Why did the Intelligent Designer design relations?

Velma Fragasso (16)
Schenectady, New York

Oh my. Aren't you the curious one, Velma. This is a difficult question, so I'm going to answer it with the insightful observation I found on the website of our member church, Kinetic Ridge Pre-Wrath Fellowship.

The Intelligent Designer made relations to reflect the mysterious spiritual relationship He will one day enjoy with all redeemed humanity following the wedding supper of the Lamb.

Does this mean the Intelligent Designer will be having relations with all of us someday, or that he's arranged for us to have dinner with a sheep after the world blows up? It's unclear, but great spiritual minds are working on this amazing mystery.

Put the pictures in the correct order according to the Intelligent Designer's sexual plan for us.

✦ RELATIONS TEST ✦

Here's a little test to help you make the right decision. Before you have any relations, ask yourself this:

"Am I doing this for my pleasure or His?"

Remember, it is always more important to pleasure Him than yourself.

Do not be impulsive and act on "animal" instinct. Even though the Intelligent Designer designed you with these feelings, you should fight them. Despite what scientists say, you are NOT an animal.

Scientists can't tell everyone what to do.

They're not the kings of the world.

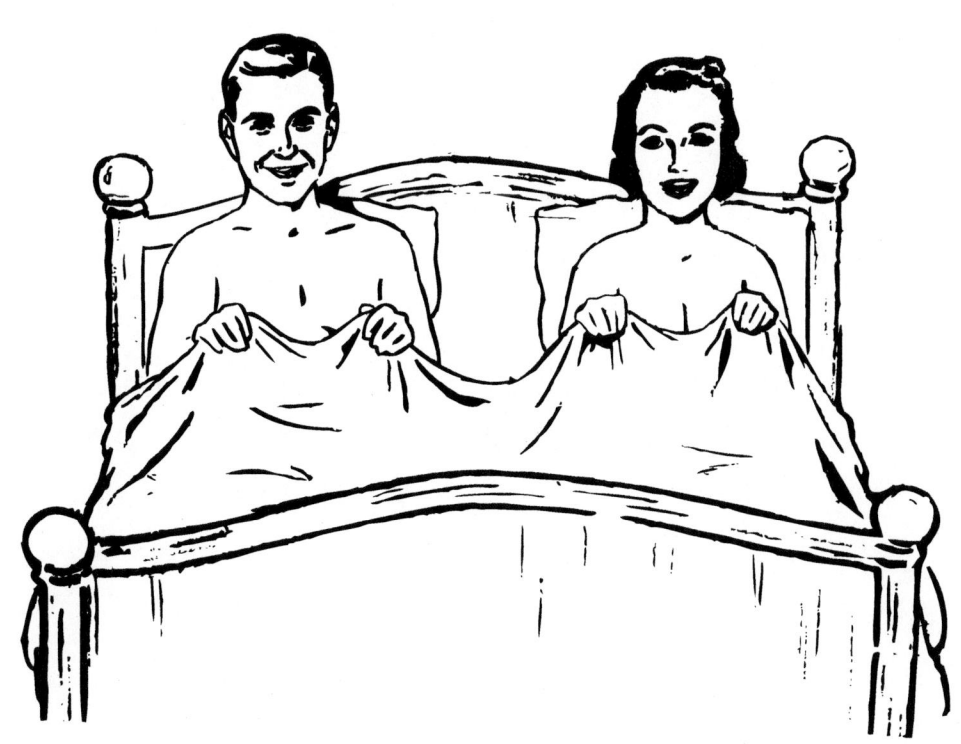

✦ MORE RELATIONS ✦

When you're having relations, you're not just having relations with your partner. You're also bringing the Intelligent Designer into the bed. You may want to think of it as a threesome with the Intelligent Designer. Or in the event you're having a threesome, then it's really a foursome.

Only you should never have a threesome because that makes the Intelligent Designer really sad. And the Intelligent Designer would never want to be in your threesome, but he always wants to be in your twosome as long as you're hetero-sexual and married. Then he can watch you and make sure you're following his rules.

In other words, a threesome is only okay when the third is our Intelligent Designer.

And, of course, <u>NO HOMOSEXUAL BEHAVIOR</u>! If you find yourself wanting to do these things, <u>DON'T</u>! Under no circumstances should you trust your feelings in the pursuit of your own happiness.

Your feelings can be wrong.

✦ A SITUATION ✦

Diana is confused and speechless.
Help put words in her mouth.

(Cut and paste your favorite response)

Let's pray together
for the Intelligent
Designer to stop making
you feel so good.

I don't hate you Stevie.
I hate the sin.
And Bobby.

You need to push those
feelings way down. All
the way back to hell.

This time you should go
to ex-gay camp without
Bobby.

It's my fault Bobby,
for challenging your
masculine authority.

Let's get married and have a
baby. You'll be cured.

Maybe I shouldn't
have tried to touch your
testicles before we were
married.

(Solution: all of these are good responses)

✦ THE END ✦

Well boys and girls, that's all we're going to have time for. We hope you appreciate the many hours of thought and research that Mrs. Schlemmer and I put into this coloring book and that it helps answer some of your questions about our amazing universe.

Speaking of a-MAZE-ing, do you like surprises? Well, you're not going to like this one.

Before the Intelligent Designer destroys the earth in the Great Tribulation as revealed in Revelations, he will anoint 144,000 servant messengers with exceptional Holy Spirit power. It says so in the Bible.

Look at the maze on the opposite page. The Intelligent Designer has already chosen 143,999 of his favorite people to get this special honor. See if you can navigate through all the burning volcanoes, floods, murder, and asteroids that our Intelligent Designer will shower upon us so that you can be the last one to receive His love before He destroys the human race. Again.

Hurry!

THE END

Book
of
Revelation

START